BALKAN
AND
MEDITERRANEAN

55 EASY RECIPES FOR FAMILY AND FRIENDS

Table of Contents

Why the Mediterranean Lifestyle?

Be with family, share with love ones, move naturally, laugh often and live more simply are the key elements of Mediterranean lifestyle, apart from famous Mediterranean diet. Unlike conventional diets, the Mediterranean diet doesn't restrict you to a daily allotment of sodium, calories or fat. Instead, it's about what you're eating, from heart-healthy unsaturated fats to satiating, high-fiber foods. Recipes maximize flavor and nutrition to create balanced plates that marry whole grains with vegetables, lean proteins, and more. Of course, you need to pay attention on portion sizes. On top of all of this deliciously nutritious eating, make sure to work physical activity into your day, especially if you have a desk job.

Based on principles below, it is easy to change healthy eating habits and really lose weight in a sustainable way. A diet is not only "stop eating carbs" —because at the end, we are all frustrated with results. No, you will not become a supermodel after four weeks, but if you accept principles of the Mediterranean diet, you will solve a problem in the long run. Moreover, you probably already know that world-leading cardiologists recommend this diet to all their patients. Yes, people in and around the Mediterranean region have much lower rates of heart diseases than those living in other parts of the world.

The Greek life philosophy everything in moderation should become your new mantra. As you can see, the base of the pyramid consists of food that should be eaten in the largest amounts (whole grains, vegetables, nuts, fruits, legumes, beans, seeds, herbs). Eat it a lot, daily. Drinking water and some physical activity every day is a must. No, you don't need to do heavy lifting at the local gym, but a 30 min. daily walk will help.

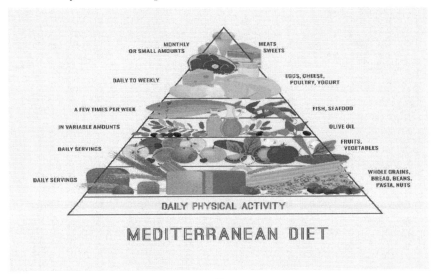

As you can see, the base of the pyramid consists of food that should be eaten in the largest amounts (whole grains, vegetables, nuts, fruits, legumes, beans, seeds, herbs). Eat it a lot, daily. Drinking water and some physical activity every day is a must. No, you don't need to do heavy lifting at the local gym, but a 30 min. daily walk will help.

The next level is reserved for fish and seafood that should be eaten 3 times a week. They will provide you with Omega-3 essential fatty acids. Poultry, eggs, and cheese are the third level, and you should consume them once a week. However, it is not a catastrophe if you eat a chicken meal twice during the week.

At the end, red meat, processed food and sweets are on the top of the pyramid and they should be consumed minimally, or not at all.

Why Balkan food?

After the fall of communism and dissolution of Yugoslavia, Balkan become (yet again?) a place with negative associations for people around the globe. If you ask anyone around the globe about positive things in the Balkans, they always mention only two things. Nice people and delicious food. "I love *sarma*," or, "Moussaka was so amazing," is something I have heard so many times. Both recipes that our mothers have made for decades and modern food. are extremely popular in the region.

The Balkans are well-known for its restaurants, but trying dishes made by someone's mother is the real thing. It is important to make dishes couple of times in order to "feel the dish" (quote by my grandmother). You can learn more and get more receipts at www.balkanfood.org or at www.facebook.com/balkanfoodonly

In general, all main dishes are served after appetizers and soup. However, every country, region, and city has its differences, and they might tell you that our version of that dish is completely different from the rest of the Balkans. My mother was almost shocked with some ingredients that others put in *sarma*, *musaka* or *pasulj*. That's the real Balkans. Enjoy!

Oatmeal with honey roasted plum

Preparation time:

> ➤ 23 minutes

Ingredients (3 servings)

- ◆ 2 cups rolled oats
- ◆ 4 halved and pitted plums
- ◆ 2 tablespoons honey
- ◆ ½ cup chopped roasted pistachios
- ◆ ¼ teaspoon salt

Preparation

Preheat oven to 375F and line a baking sheet with parchment. Place plums face-up up on baking sheet and drizzle with honey. Bake plums no more than 20 minutes, until tender and caramelized. While plums are roasting, cook oatmeal according to package directions. Portion oatmeal into bowls and top with roasted plums. Top with pistachios, and an extra drizzle of honey.

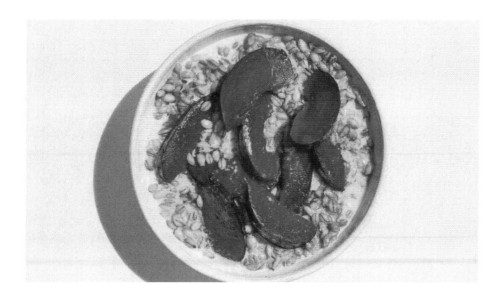

Mediterranean Frittata

Preparation time:

> 24 minutes

Ingredients (for 5 servings)

* 6 eggs
* 1/4 cup crumbled feta
* 1/2 cup milk or cream
* 1/2 cup diced tomatoes
* 1/4 cup chopped Kalamata
* olives
* 1/4 cup chopped Spanish olives
* 1 teaspoon salt
* 1 teaspoon oregano
* 1/2 teaspoon pepper

Preparation

Preheat oven to 400 degrees. Grease 8-inch pie pan or quiche dish. Whisk up all eggs and milk together until well blended. Add in remaining ingredients and mix well. Bake for no more than 20 minutes or until eggs are set.

Italian Tofu scramble

Preparation time:

> 23 minutes

Ingredients (4 servings)

- 1 package of crumbled firm tofu
- 1-2 teaspoon ground cumin
- 1 diced zucchini
- 1 bell diced pepper
- 1 diced onion
- ½ cup nutritional yeast
- 2 teaspoon tamari
- 2 teaspoon extra-virgin olive oil

Preparation

Mix first tofu, cumin, yeast and tamari with a fork. In a heavy skillet, combine pepper, zucchini, onion and olive oil. Sauté for 5 minutes. Stir in tofu mix and cook for another 10 minutes before serving.

Zucchini Pancakes
(Kolokythia Krokettes)

Preparation time:

> 65 minutes

Cook time:

> 20 minutes

Ingredients (6 servings)

- 3 cups grated zucchini
- 1 cup grated feta cheese
- 3 eggs
- 1 1/2 teaspoons minced fresh mint leaves
- 3 tablespoons flour
- 1 teaspoon salt
- Pepper
- Butter

Preparation

Mix the zucchini with salt and let stand 1 hour. Squeeze out any moisture. Beat the eggs. Add the zucchini, flour, cheese, mint, and pepper to taste. Fry 1 tablespoon at a time in butter over medium heat. Brown on both sides.

Shakshouka

Preparation time:

➢ 27 minutes

Ingredients

- 4 eggs
- 1 sliced onion
- 1 tablespoon of chopped parsley
- 2 sliced red bell peppers
- 2 chopped garlic cloves
- 1.15 oz can chopped tomatoes
- 1 teaspoon of sugar
- ¾ teaspoon of spicy harissa
- 2 tablespoons olive oil
- Salt and pepper to taste

Preparation

Heat the oil in a heavy skillet (like cast iron). Add onions and peppers and cook them until soft for about 4-5 minutes, stirring occasionally. After that, add garlic and cook for another minute. Add tomatoes, sugar and harissa and cook for about 7 minutes. Season with salt and pepper and add more harissa if you want more spice.

With wooden spoon, make 4 indentations in the mixture and add egg in each of them. Cover the pot and cook until the egg whites are just set. In total, cooking time should not be more than 20 minutes. Sprinkle with fresh parsley and serve immediately with pita bread or crusty bread.

Savory Breakfast Polenta with Eggs, Spinach and Onions

Preparation time:

➢ 20 minutes

Ingredients (2 servings)

- 2 eggs
- 1/2 cup instant polenta
- 1 cup whole milk (or milk of your choice)
- handful of spinach, stems removed
- 1/2 teaspoon salt
- 1 teaspoon butter
- 2 tablespoons Parmesan cheese
- 1 onion, sliced into thin rounds
- 1 teaspoon extra virgin olive oil
- 1 minced clove garlic
- 1 cup water
- 1/2 teaspoon balsamic vinegar

Preparation

Bring milk, water, salt, and butter to a boil, stirring often so milk doesn't scald. On low heat, add polenta, stirring continuously. Add more water depending on desired creaminess. Take off heat and add Parmesan cheese. Heat olive oil in a skillet. Add onions and sauté for about 3 minutes or until soft. Add spinach. Cook until spinach is wilted. Add garlic and balsamic vinegar. Mix well. Remove spinach and onions with a slotted spoon or tongs. Fry eggs in remaining liquid. Add salt and pepper to taste. Spread half of polenta on each plate. Spoon on half of spinach/egg mixture and then top with an egg.

Kachamak

Preparation Time:

> 5 minutes

Cook Time:

> 30 minutes

Ingredients

- 4 cups (960 ml) of water
- 2-3 teaspoon of salt
- 2/3 pound (300 gr) corn flour (or polenta)
- 2 oz (60 gr) butter (optional)

Preparation

Bring the water to the boil in a large, heavy-based saucepan over high heat. Use a wire balloon whisk to stir the water. Gradually add the polenta in a thin, steady stream, whisking constantly until all the polenta is incorporated into the water (whisking ensures the polenta is dispersed through the liquid as quickly as possible). Don't add the polenta too quickly or it will turn lumpy. Reduce heat to low (cook the polenta over low heat, otherwise it will cook too quickly and you will need to add extra water). Simmer, stirring constantly with a wooden spoon, for 10 minutes or until the mixture thickens and the polenta is soft. (To test whether the polenta is soft, spoon a little of the polenta mixture onto a small plate and set aside to cool slightly. Rub a little of the polenta mixture between 2 fingers to see if the grains have softened. If the grains are still firm, continue to cook, stirring constantly, over low heat until the polenta is soft.) Remove from heat. Add cream and butter and stir until well combined. Season to taste. Serve immediately with milk, yoghurt, sour cream, or buttermilk over it.

Domestic Broth (Domaca chorba)

Preparation time:

➢ 15 minutes

Cooking time:

➢ 45 minutes

Ingredients (5 servings)

- 3 tablespoon of oil
- 2/3 pound of veal
- 2/3 cup of rice
- 1 medium onion
- 2 carrots
- 1 cup of chopped mixed root vegetables
- Salt, pepper, parsley leaf to taste

Preparation

Fry finely chopped meat and vegetables in hot oil for a short period of time. Add about 12 cups of water and cook on medium heat for about 20 minutes. Add seasonings according to taste. Add more water if needed and cook for 15-20 minutes.

Watermelon Feta Salad

Preparation time:

> 15 minutes

Ingredients

- 35 oz seedless and cut into chunks watermelon
- 9 oz feta cheese, cut into cubes or crumbled
- Chopped bunch of mint
- 1 finely sliced small red onion
- 4 oz pitted Kalamata olives
- 1 peeled and diced small cucumber

Dressing

- 1/4 of a cup extra virgin olive oil
- 2 tablespoon lemon juice
- 1 teaspoon brown sugar
- Salt and Pepper to taste

Preparation

Remove the rind and seeds from the watermelon and cut into triangular chunks. Cut the feta cheese into small cubes, or bigger if you prefer, and place both into a large bowl. Slice the onions into paper-thin slices and add into the bowl with the rest of the ingredients. Add the chopped mint leaves, cucumber, and the Kalamata olives and set aside. In a small bowl add the olive oil, lemon juice and brown sugar and season. Whisk the ingredients to combine, taste, and adjust the seasoning. Pour the dressing over the watermelon feta salad and toss to coat. Serve immediately.

Tabouli

Preparation time:

> 29 minutes

Ingredients

- 1/2 cup fine bulgur wheat
- 1 de-stemmed bunch of parsley
- 1 bunch of sliced thinly scallions
- 1 bunch de-stemmed mint
- 3 medium diced tomatoes
- Juice of 1 lemon
- 1/3 cup extra virgin olive oil
- salt and pepper, to taste

Preparation

After washing, add bulgur to 1 cup of very hot water. Let soak for 20 minutes, while finely chopping herbs. Drain water from bulgur (1st drain and then squeeze in a colander). Add bulgur to chopped vegetables and herbs. Mix in lemon juice and olive oil. Add salt and pepper to taste.

Panedmonium salad

Preparation Time:

> ➤ 20 minutes

Ingredients

- 1 pound (450 gr) feta cheese
- ½ cup (120 ml) sour cream
- 3 large cloves garlic crushed
- 1½ teaspoons sweet or hot paprika (or to taste)
- 1 - 2 teaspoons dried chili flakes (or to taste)

Preparation

Crush the feta with a fork into a puree. Stir in sour cream to combine thoroughly with the feta. Add crushed garlic, paprika, and chili flakes. Mix well to combine. Garnish with additional paprika. Leave in the refrigerator overnight (the flavors will combine and develop during that time).

Potato Salad

Preparation time:

> 15 minutes

Ingredients (4 servings)

- 5 large potatoes
- 1 sliced large onion
- 1/2 cup diced celery
- 1/2 cup olive oil
- Chopped Parsley
- Juice of 2 lemons
- Salt and pepper

Preparation

Boil the potatoes until tender and keep hot. Slice the onion into a large bowl. Sprinkle with salt and cold water and allow to stand about 5 minutes, then drain. Slice the hot potatoes and add to the onions. Add celery, lemon juice, and olive oil. Mix well to absorb the dressing. Season to taste, and garnish with chopped parsley. Serve warm.

Mediterranean Kale Quinoa Salad

Preparation time:

> ➤ 27 minutes

Ingredients (4 servings)

- 1 cup quinoa
- 1 cup stems removed baby kale
- 3 tablespoons Kalamata olives
- 1 cup quartered cherry tomatoes
- 1 tablespoon chopped fresh parsley
- ½ cup diced cucumber
- ¼ cup minced red onion
- 2 tablespoons extra virgin olive oil
- 2 tablespoons lemon juice
- ⅛ teaspoon salt
- ⅛ teaspoon pepper
- feta cheese to taste
- 2 cups water

Preparation

Put quinoa to a medium saucepan and add water. Bring to a boil and reduce the heat to a simmer. Cook until all of the liquid is absorbed, 14-15 minutes. Meanwhile add the rest of the ingredients to a bowl and then toss in cooked quinoa. Serve with a sprinkle of feta cheese.

Syrian Ful Medames

Preparation time:

➤ 19 minutes

Ingredients (2 servings)

- 1 15 oz can fava beans
- 1/4 red onion, diced
- 1/2 tablespoon cumin
- 1 diced tomato
- 3 tablespoon tahini
- Juice of 1 lemon
- Handful of fresh chopped parley
- Extra virgin olive oil

Preparation

Put the fava beans with the liquid in a small saucepan on high heat. Bring to a boil, add cumin, salt, pepper, and lower to medium heat. Cook 9-10 minutes, stirring often. Remove from heat. Mash beans with a fork to desired consistency. Whisk together tahini and lemon juice. Add to fava beans. Mix well.

Cinnamon Chicken (Kota Kapama)

Preparation time:

> ➢ 30 minutes

Cook time:

> ➢ 40 minutes

Ingredients (4 servings)

- 8 pieces chicken
- 1/2 cup chicken stock
- 4 tablespoons butter
- 1 teaspoon finely chopped or minced garlic
- 6 fresh garden tomatoes (alternative: 1 cup chopped, drained, canned plum tomatoes)
- 2 tablespoons tomato paste
- 1 (4–inch long) cinnamon stick
- 1/4 cup extra virgin olive oil
- 1 1/2 cups finely chopped onions
- Freshly grated Parmesan cheese

Preparation

Grind some sea salt and black pepper over the chicken pieces. Heat the butter and olive oil over moderate heat in a sauté pan and brown the chicken pieces. Transfer them to a plate. Pour off all but a thin film of fat before adding the onions and garlic. Cook and stir for a few minutes until the onions are light brown.

Stir in chicken stock, tomatoes, tomato paste, cinnamon stick, 1/2 teaspoon of sea salt, and a few grindings of black pepper. Bring to a boil, and then return the chicken to the pan and baste it thoroughly with the sauce. Reduce the heat to low, cover and simmer 27-32 minutes, basting occasionally. Serve with white or brown rice or pasta. Spoon the tomato sauce over the chicken and rice or pasta. Sprinkle with Parmesan cheese, if desired.

Meatballs (Cufte)

Preparation Time:

➢ 30 minutes

Cook Time:

➢ 60 minutes

Ingredients

- 1 1/3 pounds mixed minced meat
- 1 slice of bread soaked in milk
- 1 bunch of parsley
- 2 onions
- 1 egg
- 2 tablespoons flour
- 4 tablespoons oil
- 2 cups of tomato juice
- little sugar
- 1 teaspoon ground red pepper
- salt
- pepper

Preparation

Clean onions, wash, cut, and whisk well in a wooden mortar. You can also chop onions in small pieces and then fry in a little oil, but the first method is better. Soak bread in milk and leave it to swell.

Blend together the onions with the meat, add squeezed soaked bread, and salt. Sprinkle the dried vegetables, spices, pepper, the egg, and finely chopped parsley leaf, and mix well. Leave mixture to stand twenty minutes (if you have time, can stand more) in a cool place. Moisten your hands and make meatballs. Roll them in flour and fry in hot oil until golden brown on both sides.

In the hot oil, fry 2 tablespoons of flour. Add a little ground pepper, pour tomato, and add salt and little sugar on the top of a kitchen knife, and stir sauce until thick. When the sauce is finished, drop the meatballs in sauce, and let the dish simmer slowly for 1-2 min, stirring. Serve the meatballs in sauce.

Macedonian Stuffed Peppers

Preparation Time:

➢ 30 minutes

Cook Time:

➢ 60 minutes

Ingredients

◆ 8 red peppers
◆ 1 pound (450 gr) beef/pork mincemeat combo
◆ ½ cup (120 gr) rice
◆ 1 big sliced carrot
◆ 2 chopped onions
◆ 1 egg
◆ 1 tablespoon chopped parsley salt or *Vegeta* (local mixed spice available around the globe)
◆ 1 potato or tomato to close paprika
◆ 1 cup (240 ml) of tomato paste or tomato juice
◆ 10 tablespoons of oil
◆ 2 tablespoon plain flour
◆ 1 tablespoon of ground red paprika (hot if wanted)

Preparation

Fry finely chopped onions and sliced carrots on 5 tablespoons of oil. After a few minutes, add mincemeat. Add salt, *Vegeta* to taste and continue to fry for another 5 minutes, pressing the meat with your spoon to make the pieces smaller.

Take it off the heat and add rice and an egg. Stir the mixture and spoon the mixture into the peppers to 2/3 of its height. Cover the top of each paprika with a slice of a potato or tomato, depending on what you prefer. Place peppers in a big pot or a deep pan.

In a saucepan, heat 5 tablespoons of oil and add 2 tablespoons of flour. Stir it for about 3 minutes. Quickly stir in the minced garlic and ground red paprika. Mix to a thin paste. Add the saucepan mixture paprika, add tomato juice or paste and cover it with the water. Add a little bit of *Vegeta* if desired and sprinkle chopped parsley on the top.

Put the pot into the oven and leave it for 1 hour on 475°F (250°C). You can also choose to boil it at a lower temperature for 40-45 minutes.

Bosnian Cevap

Preparation Time:

➢ 10 minutes

Cook Time:

➢ 30 minutes

Ingredients

- 3 ¼ pounds (1,5 kg) minced beef,
- ½ kg minced lamb
- 4-5 cloves of garlic
- Salt and 2 teaspoons of baking soda
- onion

Preparation

Season the meat with salt, mix it, and pour over it a ½ cup (120 ml) of water with onion, which you've cooked earlier. Mix well with your hands and leave in the fridge overnight. Grind the meat in a meat grinder twice and leave it to warm up to room temperature for a couple of hours. Then put it back in the fridge.

Before you start shaping the *cevaps*, mix in the baking soda. Mix well using your hands, and form into finger length sausages about 3/4 inch (2 cm) thick. Lightly oil the grilling surface. Grill sausages until cooked through, turning as needed, about 30 minutes.

Paprikash

Preparation time:

> ➢ 20 minutes

Cooking time:

> ➢ 60 minutes

Ingredients (5 servings)

- 2 ¼ pound of raw pork ham
- 1 pound of potatoes
- 2 onions
- 4 tablespoons of flour
- 1 teaspoon of chili flakes
- 1 tablespoon of lard
- 1 tablespoon of paprika
- 2 carrots
- Salt, Pepper, parsley leaf to taste
- 2 tomatoes
- 2 eggs

Preparation

Chop onions finely and fry them in hot lard. Once onion is golden, add chopped carrots, paprika and cubed pork. Add one glass of water and simmer at medium heat for 25-30 minutes. Add water if needed. Add cubed potatoes and enough water to cover them and cook until potatoes are soft. Add tomato, seasonings and dumplings. Cook on low heat for 4-6 minutes.

Dumplings

Whisk eggs and add flour. Use a separate dish to boil about 4 ½ cup water with a teaspoon of salt. Once the water is boiling, use the teaspoon to form dumplings and cook them until they rise to the surface.

Chicken Breast with Rosemary

Preparation time:

> ➤ 40 minutes (plus overnight)

Cooking time:

> ➤ 40 minutes

Ingredients (4 servings)

- ◆ 4 medium skinless and boneless chicken breasts
- ◆ 4 cups water
- ◆ 4 ounces feta cheese (about 1 cup crumbled)
- ◆ 2 teaspoons salt
- ◆ 2 teaspoons freshly ground black pepper
- ◆ 1 head garlic
- ◆ 6 sprigs fresh rosemary, broken into small pieces
- ◆ 1 tablespoon olive oil
- ◆ ½ large lemon
- ◆ Crostini

Preparation

Combine feta, salt, pepper, and the water in a blender and blend until smooth. Place the chicken breasts in a resealable plastic bag or container large enough to submerge the meat. Pour the brine over the chicken, cover, and refrigerate at least 8 hours or overnight.

Arrange a rack in the middle of the oven and heat to 400 F. Meanwhile, remove the chicken breasts from the brine, pat dry with paper towels, and place in a single layer in a baking dish or on an aluminum foil-lined rimmed baking sheet. Let sit for about 30 minutes at room temperature. Break off a few cloves of garlic from the head, peel, smash, and scatter around the chicken. Cut the top off the remaining garlic head to expose the cloves, cut in half horizontally, and then place the 2 pieces in the pan. Sprinkle the rosemary sprigs over the chicken, and then drizzle with the oil. Roast until an instant-read thermometer inserted in the thickest part of the breasts reads 165°F, about 40 minutes. Remove the chicken breasts from the oven, squeeze the juice from the lemon half over the chicken, and let rest for 5 minutes before serving. Squeeze the roasted garlic cloves from their peels onto crostini.

Lamb Patties with Tabbouleh

Preparation time:

> ➤ 15 minutes

Cooking time:

> ➤ 20 minutes

Ingredients (4 servings)

Tabbouleh

- ✦ 1/4 cup bulgur
- ✦ 3 seeded and diced roma tomatoes
- ✦ 1 chopped finely red onion
- ✦ 2 cup coarsely chopped parsley
- ✦ 1 cup coarsely chopped mint
- ✦ 1/3 cup olive oil
- ✦ 1/3 cup lemon juice

Patties

- ✦ 1 1/3 pound lamb mince
- ✦ 1 tablespoon finely grated lemon rind
- ✦ 2 teaspoon dried oregano
- ✦ 3 crushed clove garlic
- ✦ 1/4 cup dry breadcrumbs
- ✦ 1 lightly beaten egg
- ✦ 2 tablespoon olive oil

Preparation

Tabbouleh

Place bulgur in a large bowl. Cover with cold water. Set aside for 15 minutes until most of the water has been absorbed. Drain off excess water and fluff with a fork. Toss through onion, herbs, and tomato. Add the oil and juice and mix well. Chill until required. Serve lamb patties with tabbouleh.

Patties

In a large bowl, combine mince, breadcrumbs, egg, rind, oregano, and garlic. Season to taste. Roll the mixture into 7-8 even-sized patties. Chill for 20 minutes.

Heat the oil in a large frying pan on medium. Cook the patties in batches, for about 5 minutes each side, until browned and cooked through. Drain on a paper towel.

Green rolls (Sarmice od zelja)

Preparation Time:

> ➢ 30 minutes

Cook Time:

> ➢ 120 minutes

Ingredients

- 1 large red onion, finely chopped
- 1 pound (450 gr) ground beef
- 2 cups (460 gr) washed rice
- 1 carrot, shredded
- 20 collard green leaves
- salt and pepper
- 2 tablespoons flour
- 1 tablespoon paprika
- 4 tablespoons oil
- water
- yogurt

Preparation

Stew chopped onions for 15 minutes in a little bit of water, add ground beef, rice, and oil. Add salt and pepper to taste. If needed, add more water, as the rice will absorb most of it. Add shredded carrot and continue to stew for another 20-25 minutes (total time should be about 40-45 minutes).

While the fill is stewing, wash collard greens. Boil water in a large pot and remove from heat. Place leaves into the hot water and allow to soak for 45 minutes. Then take the leaves out of the water and use the stewed fill to make *sarma* rolls. Save this water for later use. Place *sarma* rolls vertically in a pot and make sure you fill the whole pot, so they don't fall over and unwrap. Use the leftover water from the steaming of the leaves to almost cover the *sarma* rolls in the pot.

Slow cook *sarmas* on low heat for 3 hours. When the *sarmas* are done cooking, brown some flour in oil and add a teaspoon of paprika. Add all over the top.

Cabbage dolmathes

Preparation time:

> ➢ 15 minutes

Cooking time:

> ➢ 20 minutes

Ingredients

- 1 pound ground beef
- 1 whole cabbage
- 1 minced onion
- 1/2 cup rice
- Salt
- Dill weed
- Egg lemon sauce (beat 1 egg and juice of 1 lemon with the recipe's juices in a blender until smooth)

Preparation

Boil cabbage and separate the leaves. Put the meat in a bowl and add the rice, onion, salt, and dill. Mix well. Put a bit of the mixture on each leaf and roll. Place in a cooking pot and simmer until done. Add the egg lemon sauce.

Greek Moussaka

Preparation time:

➢ 20 minutes

Cook time:

➢ 40 minutes

Ingredients

- 1 pound ground beef or lamb
- 1 large eggplant
- Vegetable oil
- 2 medium chopped onions
- 2 minced cloves garlic
- 2 egg whites
- 2 tablespoons chopped parsley
- 1 1/4 cups canned tomatoes
- 1/2 teaspoon thyme
- 1/2 teaspoon oregano
- 1/2 teaspoon nutmeg
- 1/2 cup bread crumbs
- 2 tablespoons grated Parmesan cheese
- 1/2 cup white wine
- 1 teaspoon salt

Sauce

- 2 egg yolks
- 3 tablespoons flour
- 3 tablespoons butter
- 1 1/2 cups milk
- 1/2 teaspoon salt
- 1/4 teaspoon pepper

Preparation

Pare the eggplant and cut it into 1/2–inch slices. Sprinkle with salt and set aside for 30 minutes. Rinse and dry thoroughly. Brown meat in vegetable oil with onions and garlic. Drain off the fat. Add salt, tomatoes, seasonings, parsley, and wine. Cover and cook slowly for 28-32 minutes. Cool and mix in unbeaten egg whites as well as half of the crumbs.

Brown the eggplant slices in vegetable oil. Sprinkle bottom of a 13x9 inch baking dish with remaining crumbs. Cover with the eggplant. Spoon the meat mixture over the eggplant and pour sauce over this mixture. Top with cheese and bake at 350 F for 42-48 minutes.

Sauce

Melt butter. Add flour slowly, stirring constantly. Remove from the heat and slowly stir in the milk. Return to the heat and stir until the sauce thickens. Beat the egg yolks well and gradually stir the yolks, salt, and pepper into the sauce. Blend well.

Croatian pork and sauerkraut stew (Gulash)

Preparation Time:

➢ 10 minutes

Cook Time:

➢ 60 minutes

Ingredients

- ◆ 1 ½ pounds (680 gr) pork necks without bones
- ◆ 1/3 pound (150 gr) onions
- ◆ ¼ pound (120 gr) lard
- ◆ 1 teaspoon red dried paprika
- ◆ 1 bay leaf
- ◆ 1 teaspoon caraway seed
- ◆ 1 1/2 cups (360 ml) cups white wine
- ◆ 1 ¾ pounds (780 gr) sauerkraut
- ◆ ¼ pound (120 gr) sour cream
- ◆ 1/2 teaspoon pepper
- ◆ 1 teaspoon salt
- ◆ 1 teaspoon flour (optional)

Preparation

Cut pork meat into small pieces. Finely slice onion and sauté it in lard until soft. Add meat and continue to sauté it until meat starts to change color. Add paprika and mix. Add some wine and continue to sauté it.

After 15 minutes, add sliced sauerkraut, bay leaf, caraway seeds, and more wine. If you like it really sour, add water and brine. Simmer for 35 minutes on low heat. After 20 minutes, add one teaspoon of flour and mix well. Continue to cook until sauerkraut is soft. Before serving, add sour cream and mix.

Beef and Onion Stew (Stifado)

Preparation time:

➢ 15 minutes

Cook time:

➢ 105 minutes

Ingredients (4 servings)

- 1 (2 pound) boneless tip or round beef (cut into 1–inch cubes)
- 1 medium chopped onion
- 2 cloves garlic, minced
- 1 (8 ounce) can tomato sauce
- 3 tablespoons olive oil
- 1/2 cup dry red wine
- 2 tablespoons red wine vinegar
- 1/4 teaspoon coarsely ground pepper
- Crumbled feta cheese
- 1 bay leaf
- 1 stick cinnamon
- 1 1/2 pound peeled pearl onions
- 1/2 teaspoon salt

Preparation

Cook and stir the chopped garlic and onion in oil in a Dutch oven over medium heat until the onion is tender. Remove with a slotted spoon. Cook the beef in the remaining oil about 25 minutes, stirring frequently, until all liquid is evaporated and the beef is brown on all sides. Next, drain fat. Return the onion and the garlic to the Dutch oven. Stir in all remaining ingredients except the cheese and the onions. Heat to boiling and reduce the heat. Cover and simmer 75 minutes. Add the white onions. Cover and simmer about 30 minutes until the beef and white onions are tender. Remove the bay leaf and add cinnamon. Garnish with cheese.

Karageorge steak
(Karadjordjeva shnicla)

Preparation Time:

> 10 minutes

Cook Time:

> 20 minutes

Ingredients

- 1 ¾ pounds (780 gr) of pork or veal fillet
- ¼ pounds (120 gr) of *kajmak* (see recipe for homemade *kajmak* in this cookbook)
- 1 oz (30 gr) flour
- 1 egg
- 1 oz (30 gr) breadcrumbs
- Oil
- Salt

Preparation

Slice the fillet so that you get a size-able steak. Pound the meat until it is thin and soft on both sides. Make one edge of the steak thinner so that it will stick easily one the meat is rolled up. Spread *kajmak* along the thicker edge and roll the meat into a cylinder shape. Coat the stuffed meat with flour and remove the excess flour. Then dip it into the beaten egg on all sides and then in the breadcrumbs. Roll the meat on a clean surface so that the breadcrumbs stick better. Fry in hot oil until golden yellow.

Beef and Quince Stew
(Moschari me Kydonia)

Preparation time:

➢ 15 minutes

Cooking time:

➢ 80 minutes

Ingredients (6 servings)

- 2 1/2 pounds lean boneless beef, cubed large
- 4-6 tablespoons extra virgin olive oil
- 2 large peeled, halved and sliced red onions
- 2 large peeled and cored quinces, submerged in a bowl of lemon water until ready to use
- 1/4 cup fresh chopped mint
- 1 small cinnamon stick
- 1 bay leaf
- 1/2 teaspoon ground allspice
- 3/4 cups water
- 1 cup peeled chopped plum tomatoes
- Salt and pepper to taste
- Flour for dredging

Preparation

Combine the salt, paper, and flour in a large plate and dredge the beef lightly, shaking off any excess. Heat 4 tablespoons of the olive oil in a large Dutch oven or casserole and sauté the onions over medium heat until lightly golden, about 9-10 minutes. Add the quince and sauté lightly, to color and soften a little. Remove both with a slotted spoon.

Add the remaining olive oil to the pot and brown the meat, over a high flame and turning to color on all sides. Toss the onions back into the pan, add salt, paper, allspice, tomatoes, cinnamon, bay leaf, and 3/4 cup of water. Cover, reduce heat, and simmer for 28-31 minutes. Add the quinces to the pot and continue cooking, covered, another 20-25 minutes, until the beef is tender, and the pot juices thicken. Five minutes before removing from heat, toss in the mint and adjust the seasoning with salt and pepper.

Chicken and Spinach Soup with Fresh Pesto

Preparation time:

➤ 30 minutes

Ingredients (4 servings)

- ½ cup carrot or diced red bell pepper
- 1 large boneless, skinless chicken breast, cut into quarters
- 5 cups reduced-sodium chicken broth
- 1 15-ounce can cannellini beans or great northern beans, rinsed
- 1 large minced clove garlic
- 1½ teaspoons dried marjoram
- 6 ounces baby spinach, coarsely chopped
- ¼ cup grated Parmesan cheese
- 1 tablespoon and 2 teaspoons extra-virgin olive oil, divided
- ⅓ cup lightly packed fresh basil leaves
- Freshly ground pepper to taste
- ¾ cup plain or herbed multigrain croutons for garnish (optional)

Preparation

Heat 2 teaspoons oil in a large saucepan or Dutch oven over medium-high heat. Add carrot or bell pepper and chicken. Cook about 4 minutes, turning the chicken and stirring frequently, until the chicken begins to brown. Add garlic and cook, stirring, for 1 minute more. Stir in broth and marjoram, bring to a boil over high heat. Reduce the heat and simmer, stirring occasionally, until the chicken is cooked through, about 5 minutes. With a slotted spoon, transfer the chicken pieces to a clean cutting board to cool. Add spinach and beans to the pot and bring to a gentle boil. Cook for 5 minutes to blend the flavors. Combine the remaining 1 tablespoon oil, Parmesan and basil in a food processor (a mini processor works well). Process until a coarse paste forms, adding a little water and scraping down the sides as necessary. Cut the chicken into bite-size pieces. Stir the chicken and pesto into the pot. Season with pepper. Heat until hot. Garnish with croutons, if desired.

Domestic Cooked Cabbage

Preparation Time:

> ➢ 20 minutes

Cook Time:

> ➢ 60 minutes

Ingredients

- ◆ 1 medium sized cabbage head
- ◆ 1 medium sized onion
- ◆ ¼ cup (60 gr) of rice
- ◆ 1 tablespoon and 1 teaspoon of ground red pepper
- ◆ 1 tablespoon and 2 teaspoons of a condiment (dry seasoned vegetables or *Vegeta* spice)
- ◆ 1 pound (450 gr) of pig rump meat, cut into small cubes
- ◆ 1 pound (450 gr) of smoked pork ribs
- ◆ 5-6 pieces of bacon (dry or smoked, according to taste)
- ◆ ¾ cup (180 ml) of cooked tomato (or 2 fresh tomatoes)
- ◆ 1 tablespoon of vinegar
- ◆ 5 tablespoons of cooking oil
- ◆ 1 tablespoon of flour
- ◆ 2 cups (960 ml) of water

Preparation

Place and arrange one 1/2 of the sliced cabbage onto the bottom of a 6 cups (1,4 kg) capacity cooking pan. Over the sliced cabbage, place a chopped medium sized onion and pour 50 gr of rice over the onion. Add 1 teaspoon of ground red pepper and 2 teaspoons of a dry seasoned vegetables or *Vegeta*. Place and arrange 1 pound (450 gr) of pig rump meat cut to the small pieces (cubes) over it. Place and arrange 1 pound (450 gr) of smoked ribs over the pig rump meat and 5-6 pieces of bacon over the top of the meat. Arrange the other half of the sliced cabbage over the top of these layers. Add ¾ cup of cooked tomato and 1 tablespoon of dry seasoned vegetables or "*Vegeta*.

Pour 2 cups (960 ml) of water into the pan. Turn on the stove and cooking the mixture in the pan for about 1 hour, keeping the temperature at about 400°F

(200°C). This is the approximate time for meat to be cooked. During this time, all the other ingredients will be cooked, too.

At about halfway through the cooking time, add 1 tablespoon of vinegar and keep cooking. Stir the cooking content from time to time. About 10-15 minutes before the end of cooking, lower the cooking temperature to a simmer.

Take a small saucepan, pour in 5 tablespoons of cooking oil, add 1 tablespoon of flour, fry it for a few minutes, then add 1 tablespoon of ground red pepper. Stir it well, fry it briefly, and pour this content into the main cooking pan with the cooking cabbage.

Keep cooking for about 10 minutes more. Turn off the stove, still leaving the cooking pan on it, while the plate is still hot. Prepare and arrange the dining table. Serve this warm, domestic cooked fresh cabbage as a main meal without any sides or salad, except bread, and enjoy this extraordinary taste.

Bosnian Pot Stew (Bosanski lonac)

Preparation time:

> ➢ 20 minutes

Cook time:

> ➢ 100 minutes

Ingredients

- 2-3 table spoons oil
- 1 yellow diced onion
- 2-3 garlic cloves whole (peeled and pressed)
- 2 pounds (900 gr) diced beef stew chunks
- 3 large diced carrots
- ½ pound (230 gr) green beans (cut into 1 inch pieces)
- 3 large yellow diced potatoes
- 3 large skinned and diced tomatoes
- 1 tablespoon sugar
- 1 tablespoon salt
- 1 tablespoon pepper

Preparation

Put the oil in a large pot over medium-high heat. When it's hot, add the onion, garlic, and beef, stirring occasionally for about 15 minutes. You can add a little water here and there to keep it simmering. Lower the temperature to medium, add carrots, and continue simmering. Every few minutes, add another ingredient: green beans, then potatoes, then tomatoes and sugar, all while adding a little bit of water in between.

By this time, the meat has been simmering for about 30 minutes, and the vegetables a little less. Add four cups of water (so it covers the ingredients, plus a little more). Add salt and pepper. Mix. Cover with lid offset so the stew can vent. Lower the temperature to low and cook for 90 minutes.

Roasted Black Eyed Beans with Tuna and Pancetta

Preparation time:

> ➤ 28 minutes

Ingredients (4 servings)

- ◆ 1 small jar Italian tuna
- ◆ 1 can black eyed beans
- ◆ 3 tablespoons diced, panfryed pancetta
- ◆ 1 cut in half and then sliced onion
- ◆ 1/2 teaspoon dill
- ◆ 1/4 teaspoon garlic powder
- ◆ 1/2 teaspoon Aleppo pepper
- ◆ 1/4 cup olive oil
- ◆ salt and pepper to taste

Preparation

Preheat oven to 375 F. Carefully mix together tuna, garlic powder, the black-eyed beans, onion, Aleppo pepper and dill. Place all of these ingredients in a small oven-proof casserole dish. Cover dish with olive oil, then top with pancetta. Roast for 20 minutes.

Veal with Lemon

Preparation time:

➢ 10 minutes

Cooking time:

➢ 45 minutes

Ingredients

- 1 pound veal sliced
- carrots sliced like wheels
- 1 minced onion
- 1 cup of rice
- Olive oil
- Juice of one lemon
- Pepper and Salt

Preparation

Prepare the rice in the usual way. Boil the veal slices with a bit of water. Keep removing the foam from the veal by turning the meat until it absorbs the water. Next, add the olive oil and sauté. Add the juice of lemon, pepper, and salt to taste, as well as the carrots and onion. Next, simmer for about 35 minutes. Serve it over the rice or with fries.

Croatian green peas stew with beef

Preparation Time:

> ➤ 15 minutes

Cook Time:

> ➤ 80 minutes

Ingredients

- 1 ½ pounds (680 gr) boneless lamb
- ½ pound (230 gr) onions
- 1 pound (450 gr) fresh green peas
- ½ pound (230 gr) potatoes
- 1 tablespoon lard (or 2 tablespoons oil)
- 2 teaspoons red dried paprika
- 1/2 teaspoon dried thyme
- 1 cup (240 ml) white dry wine
- 3 cups (720 ml) water
- 1 teaspoon salt
- 1/2 teaspoon pepper

Preparation

Cut meat into 1 inch (2,5 cm) large pieces. Finely mince onion and put it into a pot with lard. Sauté onion until becomes soft and transparent. Add meat and sauté until meat starts to release liquid. Add paprika, thyme, salt, and pepper and stir. Add wine and sauté until alcohol evaporates. Add some water and cook for about 30 minutes.

In the meantime, peel the potatoes, and cut it into small cubes (½ inch or 1,2 cm). Remove green peas from shuck. Add green peas and potato into stew and cook until all ingredients become soft and liquid is reduced a bit.

Pork Souvlaki with Tzatziki

Preparation time:

> ➤ 25 minutes

Cooking time:

> ➤ 20 minutes

Ingredients (4 servings)

- ◆ 1 1/4 pounds trimmed pork shoulder, cut into 3-by- 1/2-inch strips
- ◆ 1 large onion, cut through the root end into 1/2-inch wedges
- ◆ 1 cup Greek-style whole-milk yogurt
- ◆ 1/2 seeded and diced European cucumber
- ◆ 1/4 cup plus 2 tablespoons extra-virgin olive oil
- ◆ 3 tablespoons fresh lemon juice
- ◆ 2 tablespoons chopped fresh oregano
- ◆ 2 mashed garlic cloves
- ◆ Salt and Pepper
- ◆ 2 tablespoons chopped fresh mint
- ◆ Warm pita
- ◆ lemon wedges
- ◆ Tzatziki (see separate recipe in this cookbook)

Preparation

In a medium bowl, toss the pork strips and onion wedges with half of the garlic paste, olive oil, lemon juice, and chopped oregano. Season with 1 1/2 teaspoons of salt and 1/2 teaspoon of pepper. Next, let stand for 20 minutes. Meanwhile, in a bowl, mix the mint, the remaining garlic paste, the yogurt and the cucumber. Season the tzatziki with salt and pepper.

Heat a large cast-iron griddle or grill pan until very hot. Add the pork and onion wedges, along with any marinade, and cook over high heat 9-11 minutes, turning once or twice, until the pork and onion are tender. Transfer the pork and onion to plates and serve with the tzatziki, lemon wedges, and pita.

Shrimps with Feta Cheese
(Garides Me Feta)

Preparation time:

➢   10 minutes

Cook time:

➢   20 minutes

Ingredients (4 servings)

- ◆   1/2 cup minced onion
- ◆   1 1/2 tablespoons butter
- ◆   1 1/2 tablespoons vegetable oil
- ◆   1/2 cup dry white wine
- ◆   4 ripe medium peeled, seeded, and chopped tomatoes
- ◆   1 small minced clove garlic
- ◆   1 teaspoon salt
- ◆   1/4 teaspoon freshly–ground black pepper
- ◆   3/4 teaspoon oregano
- ◆   4 ounces crumbled feta cheese
- ◆   1 pound raw large shrimp (shelled and de–veined)
- ◆   1/4 cup chopped fresh parsley

Preparation

In a heavy skillet, sauté the onion in butter and oil until soft. Add wine, tomatoes, salt, pepper, garlic, and oregano. Bring to a boil, lower heat to medium, and simmer until the sauce is slightly thickened.

Stir in the cheese and simmer for 12 to 15 minutes. Adjust the seasonings. Just before serving, add the shrimp to hot sauce and cook for 5 minutes or until the shrimp are just tender. Don't overcook. Garnish with parsley and serve immediately in large bowls with crusty French bread. Pass the rice!

Shrimps with Spinach and Zucchini

Preparation time:

➢   10 minutes

Cooking time:

➢   10 minutes

Ingredients (2 servings)

- ½ pound frozen shrimps
- 1 finely chopped medium onion
- 3 finely chopped cloves of garlic
- ½ inch piece of peeled and finely chopped fresh ginger (or grated)
- 2/3 pound of fresh spinach leaves
- 1 - 2 sliced in flat rounds medium zucchini
- 2 tablespoon soy sauce
- 1 tablespoon hoisin sauce
- 2 - 3 tablespoon olive oil for stir-frying

Preparation

Heat the olive oil in a wok or a large fry-pan. Add the ginger, garlic, and onions. Cook for about 2 minutes before adding the frozen shrimp and then covering. After 3 minutes, add soy sauce and hoisin sauce. Add the zucchini, stir well and cook an additional 3 minutes. Next, add the spinach and cover. Once that spinach has wilted, stir and serve with basmati rice.

Tzatziki

Preparation time:

> 75 minutes

Ingredients

- 4 cucumbers
- 3 cloves peeled and minced garlic
- 1 tablespoon olive oil
- Salt and pepper, to taste
- 2 cups yogurt or sour cream mixed with yogurt

Preparation

Peel and seed the cucumbers and put through a fine grater (not a blender). Allow to drain in a colander until the juices have stopped running. In a small bowl, mash the garlic with salt, pepper, and the olive oil. Stir in the cucumbers and yogurt. Chill, covered, for at least 70 minutes. Serve as a dip with crackers or raw vegetables.

Kajmak

Preparation Time:

> ➢ 10 minutes

Ingredients

- ◆ 1/3 pound (150 gr) butter
- ◆ 1/3 pound (150 gr) hard feta cheese
- ◆ 1/3 pound (150 gr) sour cream

Preparation

In a bowl, whisk the butter with a fork until it's fluffy. Add crumbled feta cheese and sour cream. Mix it all well. Note: You don't need to add salt to the *kajmak* as the feta cheese is salty on its own. If you like a milder *kajmak*, add some cream.

Roasted Red Pepper Sauce (Ajvar)

Cook Time:

> 180 minutes

Ingredients

- 2 pounds (900 gr) red bell peppers (about 5 medium peppers)
- 1 medium eggplant (about 3/4 pound)
- 5 teaspoons freshly minced garlic (about 5 medium cloves)
- 1/4 cup (120 gr) sunflower or olive oil
- 1 tablespoon white vinegar
- 1 teaspoon Kosher salt
- Freshly ground black pepper, to taste

Preparation

Light one chimney full of charcoal. When all the charcoal is lit and covered with gray ash, pour out and arrange coals on one side of the charcoal grate. Set the cooking grate in place, cover the grill, and allow to preheat for 5 minutes. Clean and oil the grilling grate. Place peppers on hot side of grill and cook until blackened all over, 10-15 minutes. Transfer pepper to a large bowl, cover with plastic wrap, and let sit until cool enough to handle, about 20 minutes. Remove charred skin, seeds, and cores from peppers.

While the peppers are cooling, pierce the skin of an eggplant with a fork all over. Place the eggplant on cool side of grill. Cover and cook until skin darken and wrinkles and eggplant are uniformly soft when pressed with tongs, about 30 minutes, turning halfway through for even cooking. Remove eggplant from grill and let sit until cool enough to handle, about 10 minutes. Trim top off eggplant and split lengthwise. Using a spoon, scoop out the flesh of the eggplant, and discard the skin.

Place roasted red peppers, eggplant pulp, and garlic in a food processor fitted with a steel blade. Pulse until roughly chopped. Add in oil, vinegar, and salt, and pulse until incorporated and peppers are finely chopped.

Transfer sauce to a medium saucepan. Bring to a simmer over medium-high heat, then reduce heat to medium-low and simmer for 30 minutes, stirring occasionally. Remove from heat and season with salt and pepper to taste. Let cool to room temperature, then use immediately or transfer to an airtight container and store in refrigerator for up to two weeks.

Baked Beans (Prebranac)

Preparation Time:

➢ 10 minutes

Cook Time:

➢ 120 minutes

Ingredients

- 1 pound (450 gr) beans
- 1 ½ cups (350 ml) oil
- 2 pounds (900 gr) onion and 2 cloves of garlic
- 1 bay leaf
- Paprika powder
- Ground pepper and salt

Preparation

Put white beans in a pot, cover them water, and bring to a boil. Drain, pour hot water over them, and cook until the beans become soft. Then drain them again. Peel an onion and put it to rest in cold water for about ten minutes. Then slice it into thin rounds. Heat one part of the oil and fry the onions until they turn golden. Add a bit of ground pepper, paprika powder, and salt.

Cover the bottom of the dish with oil and then spread the beans evenly. Pour the fried onions over them. Then pour the beans again and the onions again until you run out of beans and onions. Always pour some oil on the layer of onions. The last layer has to be of beans. Put a bay leaf on top as well as two cloves of garlic and a dry, hot pepper if you wish. Then pour some oil over that. Cook in a preheated oven for about half an hour.

Cheese and Honey Pie (Melopita)

Preparation time:

➢ 30 minutes

Cook time:

➢ 40 minutes

Ingredients (8 servings)

For the filling

- 1 pound *Myzithra* cheese (soft, or ricotta cheese)
- 3 eggs (lightly beaten)
- 1/2 cup honey
- 1 lemon (the zest, grated)
- 3 teaspoon flour
- 1/4 cup sugar
- Garnish: cinnamon (ground)
- Garnish: honey

For the crust

- 1 1/4 cup flour
- 1/3 cup sugar
- 1/4 teaspoon salt
- 1 yolk from egg
- 1 teaspoon vanilla extract
- 1 tablespoon brandy or cognac
- 2 tablespoons of iced water
- 8 tablespoon (1 stick) unsalted butter, cut into 1/4-inch pieces

Preparation

➢ Preheat the oven to 350 F.

Crust

In a large mixing bowl, add flour, salt and sugar. Mix to combine. Add the butter pieces; and using two forks or a pastry blender, cut the butter into the flour. You can also use your hands for this. The mixture should resemble coarse sand when the butter is incorporated fully. Add brandy, water, egg yolk, and vanilla. Next, mix to incorporate, kneading the dough into a smooth ball. Flatten into a round disk and chill while mixing the filling.

Filling

In a medium-sized bowl, add *Myzithra* or ricotta cheese, eggs, lemon zest, honey, flour, and sugar. Mix well until all ingredients are combined. Using a rolling pin, roll out your dough to the approximate size of your baking pan. If possible, use a 10-inch tart circle with a removable bottom. You can substitute a spring form pan, a round cake pan, or even a pie dish.

Lightly grease the pan's bottom and sides. Dough should be large enough to push up the sides of your pan. The easiest way to transfer the dough from the counter to the pan is to roll it back onto your rolling pin and then unroll it over the pan. Press the dough into the sides and bottom of the pan.

Add the filling and bake in a preheated 350 F oven until the filling sets (no jiggle in the center) and it begins to turn a golden-brown color. Baking times will vary according to the size you choose to make. For a 10-inch tart, it should take 38-42 minutes. A deeper, 9-inch pie plate could take up to 45-55 minutes. Be sure to monitor your pie after 35 minutes of baking time. Serve on a plate drizzled with honey and sprinkle with ground cinnamon.

Spinach—Cheese Pie (Spankopita)

Preparation time:

> 10 minutes

Cook time:

> 20 minutes

Ingredients (8 servings)

- 2 pounds fresh spinach
- 1 finely chopped onion
- 4 tablespoons butter
- 1 cup cream sauce
- 6 beaten eggs
- 1 cup finely crumbled feta cheese
- Salt and pepper
- Dash of nutmeg
- 1/2 pound phyllo pastry sheets
- Melted Butter

Preparation

Wash the spinach and discard stems. Dry thoroughly on absorbent paper and cut into pieces. Sauté the onion in butter until soft. Add the spinach and sauté a few minutes longer. Cool and add cheese, cream sauce, eggs, and seasonings. Mix well.

Place 7 layers of phyllo pastry sheets in an 11 x 14 x 2–inch pan, brushing each sheet well with melted butter. Add the spinach mixture, then place 8 phyllo pastry sheets on filling, again buttering each sheet. Bake at 355 degrees F for 28-32 minutes, or until the crust is golden brown. Cut into small squares before serving.

Bosnian burek

Preparation Time:

➢ 40 Minutes

Cook Time:

➢ 60 Minutes

Ingredients

Pastry

- ♦ 2 cups (460 gr) of flour
- ♦ 1/2 cup (120 ml) of warm water
- ♦ 1/4 cup (60 ml) of melted butter or olive oil
- ♦ 1 egg
- ♦ Salt

Meat Filling

- ♦ 1 1/2 (680 gr) pounds of ground beef
- ♦ 1/2 cup (120 gr) of melted butter or olive oil
- ♦ 3 onions
- ♦ 2 eggs
- ♦ 2 tablespoons of paprika
- ♦ Salt and pepper

Preparation

In a large bowl, use a wooden spoon to mix together the flour, warm water, melted butter or olive oil, egg, and salt until it comes together in a doughy mass. Add more water, a tablespoon at a time, as needed to bring the ingredients together. Remove the dough to a floured work surface and knead until smooth and pliable. Cover with plastic wrap and set aside to rest for at least 30 minutes. Preheat oven to 375°F (190°C) Mix together the ground beef, onions, eggs, paprika, salt, and pepper in a large bowl until smooth and set aside.

Remove the rested dough to a lightly floured work surface and roll out into a large rectangle. Place floured fists underneath the dough and gently pull sections of the dough out to form a very thin rectangle, about 2 feet by 3 feet (60 cm x 90 cm). Take care not to tear holes in the dough. If you do, pinch them together. Let the dough rest for 10 minutes or so to dry out a little.

Brush the pastry dough all over with melted butter or olive oil. Place a row of the meat filling along the longer edge of the rolled-out pastry dough, leaving a 1 inch (2,5 cm) border. Bring the bottom of the pastry up over the meat filling and roll it up into a long, sausage-shaped roll.

Lay one end of the roll onto the middle of a greased baking pan. Carefully wrap the remainder of the pastry roll around itself to form a snail-shaped pie in the middle of the baking pan. Brush the top of the pastry with melted butter or olive oil. Place in the oven and bake for 35 to 45 minutes, or until cooked through and golden brown. Cut into wedges and serve with a large dollop of good yogurt.

Galaktoboureko

Preparation time:

> ➤ 20 minutes

Cook time:

> ➤ 50 minutes

Ingredients

- ◆ Syrup
- ◆ 3/4 cup water
- ◆ 1 cup granulated sugar
- ◆ Juice of 1 lemon
- ◆ 1 edge of orange rind
- ◆ 1 cinnamon stick

Pastry

- ◆ 2 quarts milk
- ◆ 1 cup farina
- ◆ 6 eggs
- ◆ 3/4 pound unsalted sweet butter
- ◆ 2 teaspoons vanilla extract
- ◆ 20 phyllo sheets

Preparation

Boil all syrup ingredients for 10 minutes. Cool and prepare this before making the pastry. Heat the milk to scalding. Beat the eggs until thick, add farina, and mix. Add the mixture to milk with 1/4-pound butter. Heat, stirring, until thickened. Remove from heat. Add the vanilla extract. Melt the remaining butter and butter the bottom and sides of a 10 x 14 x 2-inch pan.

Place 10 buttered phyllo leaves in the pan. Pour the farina mixture in and cover with the remaining phyllo, buttering each leaf as it's laid. Butter the top sheet very well and sculpt into diamond-shaped pieces. Bake at 350 degrees F for 50-60 minutes. Pour the cooled syrup over the hot pastry.

Gibanica

Preparation Time:

> ➢ 20 minutes

Cook Time:

> ➢ 50 minutes

Ingredients

- ✦ 1 pound (450 gr) filo pastry
- ✦ 2/3 pound (300 gr) cheese
- ✦ 2 small cups of oil
- ✦ 2 eggs
- ✦ 1 cup (240 ml) of sour cream
- ✦ Some salt if the cheese isn't salty

Preparation

Whisk eggs with some sparkling water in a bowl, then add oil and crumbled cheese. Mix it well and then add sour cream. Mix again. Oil the baking dish and line the sheets of filo pastry. First put one layer of filo pastry at the bottom of the dish, then crumble two of them, dip them in the mixture and then spread across the dish. Put one layer again, then spread two crumbled dipped ones and repeat until you run out of the mixture. Save one layer of pastry to put on top. Pour the remaining oil over the top layer. Bake in preheated oven on medium heat until golden brown.

Rice Pudding

Preparation time:

➢ 15 minutes

Cook time:

➢ 20 minutes

Ingredients (7 servings)

- 1/2 cup short grain rice
- 1 cinnamon stick
- 6 cups milk
- 1 1/2 tablespoons cornstarch mixed with 2 tablespoons milk
- 1 teaspoon vanilla extract
- 1/2 cup sugar
- Zest of 1 lemon
- A grating of fresh nutmeg
- 2 cups water
- Ground cinnamon (for garnish)

Preparation

Combine rice, cinnamon stick, and water in a saucepan and bring to a boil. Lower the heat and simmer covered for 15 minutes. Add the milk, cornstarch mixture, and sugar to the pan. Increase the heat to moderate and stir constantly 16 minutes, until the mixture thickens. Add lemon zest, vanilla extract, and nutmeg and stir to combine. Spoon into individual serving bowls or glasses and refrigerate for at least 2 hours. Dust with a little cinnamon before serving.

Pistachio and rose semolina cakes

Preparation time:

➢   15 minutes

Cooking time:

➢   50 minutes

Ingredients (20 servings)

- ◆   1 cup semolina
- ◆   ¾ cup roughly chopped pistachios
- ◆   2 cups self-rising flour
- ◆   1 teaspoon baking powder
- ◆   1 tablespoon lemon zest
- ◆   ¾ cup freshly squeezed orange juice
- ◆   6 eggs
- ◆   ½ pound softened butter
- ◆   ½ cup white sugar

Syrup

- ◆   3 ½ cups water
- ◆   1 wedge lemon
- ◆   3 cups white sugar

Icing

- ◆   1 cup icing sifted sugar
- ◆   1 tablespoon boiling water
- ◆   2 tablespoon rose water
- ◆   Rose petals
- ◆   Roughly chopped pistachios

Preparation

Preheat the oven to 325 F. Grease and line two muffin trays or petite cake trays. Prepare the syrup by bringing the water, sugar, and lemon to a boil. Lower the temperature and simmer for 10-15 minutes before removing from the heat and allowing to cool at room temperature.

Using an electric mixer, beat the butter and sugar at a high speed until pale and creamy. Add the eggs one at a time, beating after each addition. Reduce the mixer's speed and add the lemon rind and orange juice. Add the flour, semolina, and baking powder and mix until well combined. Stir the chopped pistachio nuts and transfer to a baking dish. Bake for about 30 minutes or until golden and cooked through. Remove from the oven and pour the cooled syrup over the hot cakes. Cover and allow to the syrup to absorb before removing from the baking dishes.

To make the icing, whisk the icing sugar, boiled water, and rose water in a bowl. Add more water, as necessary, since the icing should be thick and glossy. Top the cakes with a dollop of icing and sprinkle with rose petals and pistachios to garnish.

Almond Shortbread (Kourambiethes)

Preparation time:

> 10 minutes

Cook time:

> 45 minutes

Ingredients (4 servings)

- 1/2 cups blanched almonds
- 1 pound unsalted softened butter
- 1 pound confectioners' sugar
- 2 egg yolks
- 3 tablespoons of Cognac
- 1 teaspoon vanilla extract
- 3 cups cake flour
- 1/2 teaspoon baking powder

Preparation

Heat oven to 350 F. Spread the almonds in a single layer on a baking sheet. Bake, stirring occasionally, until lightly toasted, about 10 minutes. Remove from the oven, cool and chop coarsely. Beat the butter in large bowl of electric mixer on medium-high speed until very light and fluffy, 4-5 minutes. Add 3 tablespoons of the confectioners' sugar; continue beating 3 minutes. Add egg yolks, Cognac, and vanilla and beat until smooth. Beat in the almonds, flour, and baking powder until mixed well. If the dough is too soft to handle, add the additional flour. Shape the scant tablespoons full of dough between your palms into round balls or crescents.

Bake on ungreased baking sheets until set and very pale golden in color; 15 minutes. Remove the cookies to a cooling rack. Place the remaining confectioners' sugar into a sifter. While cookies are still hot, sift confectioners' sugar over the tops. Repeat twice at 20-minutes intervals.

Kadaif

Preparation time:

> ➢ 15 minutes

Cooking time:

> ➢ 100 minutes

Ingredients

Filling

- ◆ 4 cups ricotta cheese
- ◆ ½ cup heavy cream
- ◆ ½ cup milk

Syrup

- ◆ 2 tablespoons lemon juice
- ◆ 3 cups cold water
- ◆ 3 cups sugar
- ◆ 1 piece of lemon rind (optional)
- ◆ 1 stick cinnamon (optional)

Kunefe

- ◆ 1 packet Kataifi (shredded filo dough)
- ◆ 1 cup roasted and finely ground pistachio
- ◆ ¾ cup unsalted clarified butter
- ◆ 4 tablespoons rose water

Preparation

Preheat the oven to 375 F. To make the syrup, combine water, sugar, and cinnamon in a saucepan and boil for 5-6 minutes; next, then lower the heat and simmer, uncovered, for about 14-16 minutes. The syrup is ready when light yellow and when a small amount dropped onto a wooden surface is sticky or tacky when cool. Stir the lemon rind into the syrup and cool.

To make the filling, mix the cheese, milk, and heavy cream together well.

To assemble kadaif, brush the inside of a 10x15x2 inch baking dish all over with a little of the clarified butter. Separate the shredded dough in half by holding up and pulling it apart. Spread half the dough evenly in the pan. Dip a wide pastry brush into butter and drizzle half the butter over the dough. Spread the filling over the pastry evenly. Place the other half of the shredded dough over the kadaif and gently press down all over. Drizzle any remaining butter over the dough.

Bake the kadaif in the center of the preheated oven for 33-37 minutes, until golden. Remove from the oven and immediately pour over the rosewater, followed by the cooled syrup. Cover the kadaif and allow the pastry to absorb the syrup. Sprinkle with roasted, ground pistachio nuts. Serve warm or cool to room temperature.

Baklava

Preparation Time:

- ➢ 60 minutes

Cook Time:

- ➢ 75 minutes

Ingredients

- ◆ 1 pound (450 gr) package phyllo (filo) dough thawed according to package instructions
- ◆ 2 1/2 sticks (1/4 cups or 290 gr) melted unsalted butter
- ◆ 1 pound (450 gr) walnuts, finely chopped
- ◆ 1 tablespoon ground cinnamon
- ◆ 1 cup (230 gr) granulated sugar
- ◆ 2 tablespoons lemon juice (juice of 1/2 lemon)
- ◆ 3/4 cup (180 ml) water
- ◆ 1/2 cup (120 ml) honey
- ◆ Melted chocolate chips and chopped walnuts for garnish (optional)

Preparation

Thaw phyllo dough according to package instructions (this is best done overnight in the fridge, then place it on the counter for 1 hour before starting your recipe to bring it to room temperature). Trim phyllo dough to fit your baking sheet. The best phyllo dough package is with 2 rolls with a total of 40 sheets that measured 9×14, so I had to trim them slightly. You can trim one stack at a time then cover with a damp towel to keep the dough from drying out.

Butter the bottom and sides of a 13×9 non-stick baking pan. In a medium saucepan, combine 1 cup (230 gr) sugar, 1/2 cup (120 ml) honey, 2 tablespoons lemon juice, and 3/4 cup (180ml) water. Bring to a boil over medium high heat, stirring until the sugar is dissolved, then reduce heat to medium low and boil an additional 4 minutes without stirring. Remove from heat, and let the syrup cool while preparing the filling.

Preheat Oven to 325°F (160°C). Pulse walnuts about 10 times in a food processor until coarsely ground/finely chopped. In a medium bowl, stir together: 1 pound (450 gr) finely chopped walnuts and 1 tablespoon cinnamon. Place 10 phyllo sheets into the baking pan one at a time, brushing each sheet with butter once it's in the pan before adding the next (i.e. place phyllo sheet into pan, brush the top with butter, place next phyllo sheet in pan, butter the top etc.)

Always keep the remaining phyllo covered with a damp towel. Spread about 1/5 of nut mixture (about 3/4 cup) over phyllo dough. Add 5 buttered sheets of phyllo, then another layer of nuts. Repeat 4 times. Finish off with 10 layers of buttered phyllo sheets. Brush the top with butter. **Here's the order**:

- ➢ 10 buttered phyllo sheets, 3/4 cup (180 gr) nut mixture
- ➢ 5 buttered phyllo sheets, 3/4 cup (180 gr) nut mixture
- ➢ 5 buttered phyllo sheets, 3/4 cup (180 gr) nut mixture
- ➢ 5 buttered phyllo sheets, 3/4 cup (180 gr) nut mixture
- ➢ 5 buttered phyllo sheets, 3/4 cup (180 gr) nut mixture
- ➢ 10 buttered phyllo sheets and butter the top

Cut pastry into 1 1/2″ wide strips, then cut diagonally to form diamond shapes. Bake at 325°F (160°C) for 1 hour and 15 min or until the top is golden brown. Remove from oven and immediately spoon the cooled syrup evenly over the hot baklava (you'll hear it sizzle). This will ensure that it stays crisp rather than soggy. Let the baklava cool completely uncovered and at room temperature. For best results, let baklava sit 4-6 hours or overnight at room temperature for the syrup to penetrate and soften the layers. Garnish baklava with finely chopped nuts or drizzle with melted chocolate. Store at room temp, covered with a tea towel for 1 to 2 weeks.

Tulumbe

Preparation Time:

> ➤ 15 minutes

Cook Time:

> ➤ 30 minutes

Ingredients

- ◆ 2 tablespoons butter or 2 tablespoons margarine, melted
- ◆ 1 cup (230 gr) flour
- ◆ 3 tablespoons water
- ◆ 4 eggs
- ◆ 1⁄2 teaspoon salt
- ◆ 1 1⁄4 cups (300 ml) olive oil, for frying

Syrup

- ◆ 2 cups (460 gr) sugar
- ◆ 1 3⁄4 cups (420 ml) water
- ◆ 1 teaspoon lemon juice

Preparation

Syrup

Put the sugar, water, and lemon juice into a saucepan, and after melting the sugar by stirring, allow it to boil until moderately thick. Set aside to cool.

Pastry

Heat the margarine in a saucepan, add the water and salt, and bring to a boil. Reduce heat and add the flour at once. Stir the mixture constantly with a wooden spoon and continue until the mixture pulls away from the sides of the pan and forms a ball. This should take 6 minutes. Then remove the pan from the heat and set aside to cool. When cool, add the eggs and knead for approximately 10 minutes. Using a pastry bag with a large nozzle or a serrated spoon, put 7-8 pastries in a pan containing the heated olive oil. Start frying the pastry over low heat, increase heat when pastry puffs up a bit, and fry until golden. Remove the fried pastry with a slotted spoon, draining away the oil, then put into the syrup. Strain off the syrup, place the tulumba on serving plate, and serve when cool.

Vanila Slice (Krempita)

Preparation time:

> ➢ 20 minutes

Cooking time:

> ➢ 30 minutes

Ingredients (25 servings)

- ◆ 12 cups of milk
- ◆ 1 sachet of vanilla sugar
- ◆ 8 eggs
- ◆ 4/5 pound sugar
- ◆ ½ pound white flour
- ◆ 1 package of puff pastry sheets

Preparation

Spread puff pastry sheets to form two identical dough sheets that fit pan shape, and bake them in the oven separately. Before baking, make square slashes with a knife across the top surface of the pastry sheet prepared for upper crust to facilitate slicing and pastry sheet for bottom crust prick all over with a fork to make sure that the crust doesn't puff.

Put milk and a sachet of vanilla sugar into a saucepan and boil. Meanwhile, put 8 egg yolks and 2/3 pound of sugar in separate saucepan and whisk, then add ½ pound of flour and stir with a wire whisk. Slowly pour over boiled milk, stirring gently and constantly mixture with a wire whisk. Steam cream, stirring constantly and when it becomes thick, add snow made of 6 beaten egg whites and 1 cup of sugar. Using a wire whisk, quickly stir well mixture, remove the pan from the stove, pour cream over the bottom crust and spread, and then cover it with the top crust. Leave it to cool, then cut vanilla slice into square pieces and sprinkle with powdered sugar over the top.

Avocado and pumpkin muffins

Preparation time:

> 21 minutes

Ingredients (12 servings)

- 2 eggs
- 1/2 cup mashed avocado
- 1 1/2 cup pumpkin puree
- 2 cups flour
- 1 cup sugar
- 1 teaspoon baking soda
- 1 teaspoon salt
- 1 teaspoon cinnamon
- 1 teaspoon vanilla extract
- 1/2 cup of chopped walnuts

Preparation

Preheat oven to 375 F. Grease a muffin tin or line with paper cups. In a large bowl, mix pumpkin, avocado and eggs.

In a separate bowl, whisk sugar, flour, baking soda, salt, cinnamon and vanilla. Combine with avocado mixture, but do not over-mix. Stir in walnuts. Spoon batter into prepared muffin tin and bake for no more than 18 minutes or until tops start to brown and a knife inserted into a muffin comes out clean.

Lemon cake

Preparation time:

18 minutes

Ingredients (11 servings)

- 4 eggs
- 1/2 cup milk
- 1 cup sugar
- 1/2 cup sunflower oil
- 2 cups flour
- 1 tablespoon baking powder
- 1/2 teaspoon salt
- 2 tablespoon fresh lemon juice
- 2 tablespoon lemon zest
- 1/2 teaspoon vanilla extract

Preparation

Whisk eggs and sugar until light and creamy. Gently add in the flour, sunflower oil, flour, baking powder, salt, and milk. Beat until smooth, then add in vanilla and lemon juice and zest.

Pour the batter into a prepared 10-inch tube pan and bake in a preheated to 350 F oven for about 40 minutes, or until a toothpick comes out clean. Set aside to cool then turn onto a wire rack to finish cooling.

One last thing

If you enjoyed this book or found it useful, I'd be very grateful if you'd post a short review. Your support really does make a difference and I read all the reviews personally, so I can apply your feedback and make this book even better.

Thanks again for your support!

Please send me your feedback at Amazon or at:

www.facebook.com/balkanfoodonly

www.balkanfood.org

Printed in Great Britain
by Amazon

35029204R00047